Albert Schweitzer

THE LIGHT WITHIN US

p. 59

Albert Schweitzer

THE
LIGHT
WITHIN
US

THE WISDOM LIBRARY

A Division of

THE PHILOSOPHICAL LIBRARY
New York

The selections contained in this little volume were made
by Richard Kik. The original German edition *Vom Licht
in uns* was published by Verlag J. F. Steinkopf, Stutt-
gart; this edition by courtesy of Verlag J. F. Steinkopf
as well as C. H. Beck Verlag, Munich and Richard
Meiner Verlag, Hamburg.

Type set by *The Polyglot Press*, New York
Manufactured in the United States of America

Albert Schweitzer

THE LIGHT WITHIN US

THE BEGINNING OF ALL spiritual life is fearless belief in truth and its open confession. V–63

❦

EVERYTHING deep is also simple and can be reproduced simply as long as its reference to the whole truth is maintained.

V–7

❦

BUT what matters is not what is witty but what is true. In this case the simple thing is the truth, the uncomfortable truth with which we have to work. V–23

❦

I INTENTIONALLY avoid technical philosophical phraseology. My appeal is to thinking men and women whom I wish to provoke to elemental thought about the questions of existence which occur to the mind of every human being. O–199

ALWAYS accustomed in French to be careful about the rhythmical arrangement of the sentence, and to strive for simplicity of expression, these things have become equally a necessity to me in German. And now through my work on the French *Bach* it became clear to me what literary style corresponded to my nature.   O—63

❦

THE DIFFERENCE between the two languages, as I feel it, I can best describe by saying that in French I seem to be strolling along the well-kept paths in a fine park, but in German to be wandering at will in a magnificent forest. Into literary German there flows continually new life from the dialects with which it has kept in touch. French has lost this ever fresh contact with the soil. It is rooted in its literature, becoming thereby, in the favorable, as in the unfavorable sense of the word, something finished, while German in the same sense remains something unfinished. The perfection of French consists in being able to express a thought in the clearest and most concise way; that of German in being able to present it in its manifold aspects. As the greatest linguistic creation in French I count Rousseau's *Contrat Social*. What is nearest perfection in German I see in Luther's translation of the Bible and Nietzsche's *Jenseits von Gut und Boese* ("Beyond Good and Evil").

O—62-63

❦

WHEN I look back upon my early days I am stirred by the thought of the number of people whom I have to thank for what they gave me or for what they were to me. At the same time I am haunted by an oppressive consciousness of the little gratitude I really showed them while I was young. How many of them have said farewell to life without my having made clear to them what it meant to me to receive from them so much kindness or so much care! Many a time have I, with a feeling of shame, said quietly to myself over a grave the words which my mouth ought to have spoken to the departed, while he was still in the flesh.

M—65

❦

IN THE same way we ought all to make an effort to act on our first thoughts and let our unspoken gratitude find expression.

Then there will be more sunshine in the world, and more power to work for what is good. But as concerns ourselves we must all of us take care not to adopt as part of our theory of life all people's bitter sayings about the ingratitude in the world. A great deal of water is flowing underground which never comes up as a spring. In that thought we may find comfort. But we ourselves must try to be the water which does find its way up; we must become a spring at which men can quench their thirst for gratitude.   M—66

❦

IN MY first years at Mülhausen I suffered much from a homesick longing for the church at Günsbach; I missed my father's sermons, and the services I had been famil·iar with all my life.

The sermons used to make a great impression on me, because I could see how much of what my father said in the pulpit was of a piece with his own life and experience. I came to see what an effort, I might say what a struggle, it meant for him to open his heart to the people every Sunday. I still remember sermons I heard from him while I was at the village school.

But what I loved best was the afternoon service, and of these I hardly ever missed a single one when I was in Günsbach. In the deep and earnest devotion of those services the plain and homely style of my father's preaching showed its real value, and the pain of thinking that the holy day was now drawing to its close gave these services a peculiar solemnity.

From the services in which I joined as a child I have taken with me into life a feeling for what is solemn, and a need for quiet and self-recollection, without which I cannot realize the meaning of my life. I cannot, therefore, support the opinion of those who would not let children take part in grown-up people's services till they to some extent understand them. The important thing is not that they shall understand, but that they shall feel something of what is serious and solemn. The fact that the child sees his elders full of devotion, and has to feel something of their devotion himself, that is what gives the service its meaning for him.

M—44-45

THERE was another incident of my earliest childhood which I remember as the first occasion on which I consciously, and on account of my own conduct, felt ashamed of myself. I was still in petticoats, and was sitting on a stool in the yard while my father was busy about the beehives. Suddenly a pretty little creature settled on my hand, and I watched it with delight as it crawled about. Then all at once I began to shriek. The pretty little creature was a bee, which had a good right to be angry when the pastor was robbing him of the honey-filled combs in his hive, and to sting the robber's little son in revenge! My cries brought the whole household round me, and everyone pitied me. The servant girl took me in her arms and tried to comfort me with kisses, while my mother reproached my father for beginning to work at the hives without first putting me in a place of safety. My misfortune having made me so interesting an object, I went on crying with much satisfaction, till I suddenly noticed that, although the tears were still pouring down, the pain had disappeared. My conscience told me to stop, but in order to be interesting a bit longer I went on with my lamentations, so getting a lot more comforting than I really needed. However, this made me feel such a little rogue that I was miserable over it all the rest of the day. How often in after life, when assailed by temptation, has this experience warned me against exaggeration, or making too much of, whatever has happened to me!

M—3-4

❧

ON THIS, my first meeting with an author, there followed a second and greater experience. A Jew from a neighbouring village, Mausche by name, who dealt in land and cattle, used to come occasionally through Günsbach with his donkey-cart. As there was at that time no Jew living in the village, this was always something of an event for the boys; they used to run after him and jeer at him. One day, in order to announce to the world that I was beginning to feel myself grown up, I could not help joining them, although I did not really understand what it all meant, so I ran along with the rest behind him and his donkey-cart, shouting: "Mausche, Mausche!" The most daring of them used to fold the corner of their shirt or jacket to look like a pig's ear, and spring with that as close to him as they could. In this way we followed him out of the village as far as the bridge, but Mausche, with his freckles and his grey beard, drove on as unperturbed as his donkey, except that he several times turned round and looked at us with an embarrassed but good-natured smile. This smile overpowered me. From Mausche it was that I first learnt what it means to keep silent under persecution, and he thus gave me a most valuable lesson. From that day forward I used to greet him politely, and later, when I was in the secondary school (the Gymnasium) I made it my practice to shake hands and walk a little way along with him, though he never learnt what he really was to me. He had the reputation of being a usurer and a property-jobber, but I never tried to find out whether this was true or not. To me he has always been just "Mausche" with the tolerant smile, the smile which even to-day compels me to be patient when I should like to rage and storm.

M—8-9

❦

ALL my life I have been glad that I began in the village school. It was a good thing for me that in the process of learning I had to measure myself with the village boys, and thus make it quite clear to myself that they had at least as much in their heads as I had in mine. I was never a victim of that ignorance which afflicts so many of the boys who go straight to a Gymnasium, and there tell each other that the children of the educated classes have more in them than the lads who go to school in darned stockings and wooden clogs. Even to-day if I meet any of my old schoolfellows in the village or on a farm, I at once remember vividly the points in which I did not reach their level. One was better at mental arithmetic; another made fewer mistakes in his dictation; a third never forgot a date; another was always top in geography; another I mean you, Fritz Schoppeler—wrote almost better than the schoolmaster. Even to-day they stand in my mind for the subjects in which they were at that time superior to me.   M—21

THAT a deep sense of duty, manifested in even the smallest matters, is the great educative influence, and that it accomplishes what no exhortations and no punishments can, has, thanks to him, become with me a firm conviction, a conviction the truth of which

I have ever tried to prove in practice in all that I have had to do as an educator.   M–39-40

🌿

THEN a saviour appeared for me in the person of a new form-master, Dr. Wehmann by name. In the course of the first few days I saw clearly through the mist of my dreaminess this fact; our new teacher came with every lesson carefully prepared; he knew exactly how much of the subject he wanted to take, and he got through that amount. He also gave us back our fair-copy exercise books on the proper day, and in the proper lesson hour. Experience of this self-disciplined activity had a distinct effect upon me. I should have been ashamed to incur his pleasure, and he became my model. Three months later when my form, the Quarta, got its Easter report, I was on of the better scholars, although my Christmas report had been so bad that my mother had gone about the whole of the Christmas holidays with eyes that were red from crying.   M–39

🌿

IN THE education and the school books of to-day the duty of humanity is relegated to an obscure corner, as though it were no longer true that it is the first thing necessary in the training of personality, and as if it were not a matter of great importance to maintain it as a strong influence in our human race against the influence of outer circumstances.

D-26

AS FAR back as I can remember I was saddened by the amount of misery I saw in the world around me. Youth's unqualified *joie de vivre* I never really knew, and I believe that to be the case with many children, even though they appear outwardly merry and quite free from care.

One thing that specially saddened me was that the unfortunate animals had to suffer so much pain and misery. The sight of an old limping horse, tugged forward by one man while another kept beating it with a stick to get it to the knacker's yard at Colmar, haunted me for weeks.

It was quite incomprehensible to me—this was before I began going to school—why in my evening prayers I should pray for human beings only. So when my mother had prayed with me and had kissed me goodnight, I used to add silently a prayer that I had composed myself for all living creatures. It ran thus: "O, heavenly Father, protect and bless all things that have breath; guard them from all evil, and let them sleep in peace." M—27-28

❦

FROM my mother I also inherited a terribly passionate temper, which she again had inherited from her father, who was a very good man but very quick-tempered. My disposition showed itself in games; I played every game with terrible earnestness, and got angry if anyone else did not enter into it with all his might. When I was nine or ten years old I struck my sister Adela, because she was a very slack opponent in a game, and through her indifference let me win a very easy victory. From that time onwards I began to feel anxious about my passion for play, and gradually gave up all games. I have never ventured to touch a playing-card. I also, on January 1, 1899, when I was a student, gave up for ever the use of tobacco. M—23

❦

FROM experiences like these, which moved

my heart and often made me feel ashamed, there slowly grew up in me an unshakeable conviction that we have no right to inflict suffering and death on another living creature unless there is some unavoidable necessity for it, and that we ought all of us to feel what a horrible thing it is to cause suffering and death out of mere thoughtlessness. And this conviction has influenced me only more and more strongly with time. I have grown more and more certain that at the bottom of our heart we all think this, and that we fail to acknowledge it and to carry our belief into practice chiefly because we are afraid of being laughed at by other people as sentimentalists, though partly also because we allow our best feelings to get blunted. But I vowed that I would never let my feelings get blunted, and that I would never be afraid of the reproach of sentimentalism.

M—31

❦

THE THOUGHT that I had been granted such a specially happy youth was ever in my mind; I felt it even as something oppressive, and ever more clearly there presented itself to me the question whether this happiness was a thing that I might accept as a matter of course. Here, then, was the second great experience of my life, viz. this question about the right to happiness. As an experience it joined itself to that other one which had accompanied me from my childhood up; I mean my deep sympathy with the pain which prevails in the world around us. These two experiences slowly melted into one another, and thence came definiteness to my interpretation of life as a whole, and a decision as to the future of my own life in particular.

It became steadily clearer to me that I had not the inward right to take as a matter of course my happy youth, my good health, and my power of work. Out of the depths of my feeling of happiness there grew up gradually within me an understanding of the saying of Jesus that we must not treat our lives as being for ourselves alone. Whoever is spared personal pain must feel himself called to help in diminishing the pain of others. We must all carry our share of the misery which lies upon the world.   M–60-61

THE FORMATION of drops of rain, of

snowflakes, and of hailstones had always been a special puzzle to me. It hurt me to think that we never acknowledge the absolutely mysterious character of Nature, but always speak so confidently of explaining her, whereas all that we have really done is to go into fuller and more complicated descriptions, which only make the mysterious more mysterious than ever. Even at that age, it became clear to me that what we label Force or "Life" remains it its own essential nature for ever inexplicable.

Thus I fell gradually into a new habit of dreaming about the thousand and one miracles that surround us, though fortunately the new habit did not, like my earlier thoughtless day-dreams, prevent me from working properly. The habit, however, is with me still, and gets stronger. If during a meal I catch sight of the light broken up in a glass jug of water into the colours of the spectrum, I at once become oblivious of everything around me, and unable to withdraw my gaze from the spectacle. M—52-53

BUT HOW often do I inwardly rebel! How much I suffer from the way we spend so much of our time uselessly instead of talking in serious-wise about serious things, and getting to know each other well as hoping and believing, striving and suffering mortals!   M—56

℘

IF I meet people to whom it is impossible to open oneself out as a man who thinks, I feel a passionate enjoyment in their society as if I were as young as ever, and if I stumble on a young man who is ready for serious discussion, I give myself up to a joyous exchange of cut and thrust which makes the difference between our ages, whether for good or ill, a thing of no account.   M—56

℘

I ALWAYS think that we live, spiritually, by what others have given us in the significant hours of our life. These significant hours do not announce themselves as coming, but arrive unexpected. Nor do they make a great show of themselves; they pass almost unperceived. Often, indeed, their significance comes home to us first as we look back, just as the beauty of a piece of music or of a landscape often strikes us first in our recollection of it. Much that has become our own in gentleness, modesty, kindness, willingness to forgive, in veractiy, loyalty, resignation under suffering, we owe to people in whom we have seen or experienced these virtues at work, sometimes in a great matter, sometimes in a small. A thought which had become act sprang into us like a spark, and lighted a new flame within us.

I do not believe that we can put into anyone ideas which are not in him already. As a rule there are in everyone all sorts of good ideas, ready like tinder. But much of this tinder catches fire, or catches it successfully, only when it meets some flame or spark from outside, *i.e.* from some other person. Often, too, our own light goes out, and is rekindled by some experience we go through with a fellow-man. Thus we have each of us cause to think with deep gratitude of those who have lighted the flames within us.   M—67-68

❦

SIMILARLY, not one of us knows what effect his life produces, and what he gives to others; that is hidden from us and must remain so, though we are often allowed to see some little fraction of it, so that we may not lose courage. The way in which power works is a mystery. M—68

❦

TO THIS fact, that we are each a secret to the other, we have to reconcile ourselves. To know one another cannot mean to know everything about each other; it means to feel mutual affection and confidence, and to believe in one another. A man must not try to force his way into the personality of another. To analyse others—unless it be to help back to a sound mind someone who is in spiritual or intellectual confusion—is a rude commencement, for there is a modesty of the soul which we must recognize, just as we do that of the body. The soul, too, has its clothing of which we must not deprive it, and no one has a right to say to another: "Because we belong to each other as we do, I have a right to know all your thoughts." Not even a mother may treat her child in that way. All demands of that sort are foolish and unwholesome. In this matter giving is the only valuable process; it is only giving that stimulates. Impart as much as you can of your spiritual being to those who are on the road with you, and accept as something precious what comes back to you from them.

M—69

❧

WE MUST all beware of reproaching those we love with want of confidence in us if they are not always ready to let us look into all the corners of their heart. We might almost say that the better we get to know each other, the more mystery we see in each other. Only those who respect the personality of others can be of real use to them.

I think, therefore, that no one should compel himself to show to others more of his inner life than he feels is natural to show. We can do no more than let others judge for themselves what we inwardly and really are, and do the same ourselves with them. The only essential thing is that we strive to have light in ourselves. Our strivings will be recognized by others, and when people have light in themselves, it will shine out from them. Then we get to know each other as we walk together in the darkness, without needing to pass our hands over each other's faces, or to intrude into each other's hearts.

M—70

OUR HUMAN atmosphere is much colder than it need be, because we do not venture to give ourselves to others as heartily as our feelings bid us. M—72

WE MUST, indeed, take care to be tactful, and not mix ourselves up uninvited in other people's business. On the other hand we must not forget the danger lurking in the reserve which our practical daily life forces on us. We cannot possibly let ourselves get frozen into regarding everyone we do not know as an absolute stranger. No man is ever completely and permanently a stranger to his fellow-man. Man belongs to man. Man has claims on man. Circumstances great or small may arise which make impossible the aloofness which we have to practise in daily life, and bring us into active relations with each other, as men to men. The law of reserve is condemned to be broken down by the claims of the heart, and thus we all get into a position where we must step outside our aloofness, and to one of our fellow-men become ourselves a man. M—71-72

THE CONVICTION that in after life we must struggle to remain thinking as freely and feeling as deeply as we did in our youth, has accompanied me on my road through life as a faithful adviser. Instinctively I have taken care not to become what is generally understood by the term, a man of ripe experience (ein reifer Mensch).

The epithet "ripe" applied to persons always did, and does still, convey to me the idea of something depressing. I hear with it, like musical discords, the words, impoverishment, stunted growth, blunted feelings. What we are usually invited to contemplate as "ripeness" in a man is the resigning of ourselves to an almost exclusive use of the reason. One acquires it by copying others and getting rid, one by one, of the thoughts and convictions which were dear in the days of one's youth. We believed once in the victory of truth; but we do not now. We believed in our fellow-men; we do not now. We believed in goodness; we do not now. We were zealous for justice; but we are not so now. We trusted in the power of kindness and peaceableness; we do not now. We were capable of enthusiasm; but we are not so now. To get through the shoals and storms of life more easily we have lightened our craft, throwing overboard what we thought could be spared. But it was really our stock of food and drink of which we deprived ourselves; our craft is now easier to manage, but we ourselves are in decline.

M—73-74

AS ONE who tries to remain youthful in his thinking and feeling, I have struggled against facts and experience on behalf of belief in the good and the true. At the present time when violence, clothed in life, dominates the world more cruelly than it ever has before, I still remain convinced that truth, love, peaceableness, meekness, and kindness are the violence which can master all other violence. The world will be theirs as soon as ever a sufficient number of men with purity of heart, with strength, and with perseverance think and live out the thoughts of love and truth, of meekness and peaceableness.

The knowledge of life, therefore, which we grown-ups have to pass on to the younger generation will not be expressed thus: "Reality will soon give way before your ideals," but "Grow into your ideals, so that life can never rob you of them." If all of us could become what we were at fourteen, what a different place the world would be! M–77

❧

ONLY a person who can find a value in every sort of activity and devote himself to each one with full consciousness of duty, has the inward right to take as his object some extraordinary activity instead of that which naturally falls to his lot. Only a person who feels his preference to be a matter of course, not something out of the ordinary, and who has not thought of heroism, but just recognizes a duty undertaken with sober enthusiasm, is capable of becoming a spiritual adventurer such as the world needs. There are no heroes of action: only heroes of renunciation and suffering. Of such there are plenty. But few of them are known, and even these not to the crowd, but to the few. O–91

❧

THREE times a week, from eleven to twelve, when the morning lessons were over,

I had to take the Confirmation classes for boys, which in Alsace continue for two years. I tried hard to give them as little home work to do as possible, that the lessons might be a time of pure refreshment for heart and spirit. I therefore used the last ten minutes for making them repeat after me, and so get to know by heart, Bible sayings and verses of hymns which they might take away from these classes to guide them throughout their lives. The aim of my teaching was to bring home to their hearts and thoughts the great truths of the Gospel, and to make them religious in such a way that in later life they might be able to resist the temptations to irreligion which would assail them. I tried also to awake in them a love for the Church, and a feeling of need for a solemn hour for their souls in the Sunday services. I taught them to respect traditional doctrines, but at the same time to hold fast to the saying of St. Paul that where the spirit of Christ is, there is liberty.

Of the seed which for years I was thus sowing, some has taken root and grown, as I have been privileged to learn. Men have thanked me for having then brought home to their hearts the fundamental truths of

the religion of Jesus as something to be ab-
sorbed into one's thought, and having thus
strengthened them against the danger of giving up all religion in later life.   O—27-28

❦

GROWN-UP people reconcile themselves
too willingly to a supposed duty of prepar-
ing young ones for the time when they will
regard as illusion what now is an inspira-
tion to heart and mind. Deeper experience
of life, however, advises their inexperience
differently. It exhorts them to hold fast,
their whole life through, to the thoughts
which inspire them. It is through the idealism of youth that man catches sight of truth,
and in that idealism he possesses a wealth
which he must never exchange for anything
else.   M—75

❦

THAT ideals, when they are brought into
contact with reality, are usually crushed by
facts does not mean they are bound from
the very beginning to capitulate to the facts,
but merely that our ideals are not strong
enough; and they are not strong enough because they are not pure and strong and
stable enough in ourselves.

❧§ 25

The power of ideals is incalculable. We see no power in a drop of water. But let it get into a crack in the rock and be turned to ice, and it splits the rock; turned into steam, it drives the pistons of the most powerful engines. Something has happened to it which makes active and effective the power that is latent in it.   M—75

❧

IDEALS are thoughts. So long as they exist merely as thoughts, the power latent in them remains ineffective, however great the enthusiasm, and however strong the conviction with which the thought is held. Their power only becomes effective when they are taken up into some refined human personality.

The ripeness, then, that our development must aim at is one which makes us simpler, more truthful, purer, more peace-loving, meeker, kinder, more sympathetic. That is the only way in which we are to sober down with age. That is the process in which the soft iron of youthful idealism hardens into the steel of a full-grown idealism which can never be lost.   M—75-76

NO ONE who is always striving to refine his character can ever be robbed of his idealism, for he experiences in himself the power of the ideals of the good and the true.

M—76-77

❧

ALL acts and facts are a product of spiritual power, the successful ones of power which is strong enough; the unsuccessful ones of power which is too weak. Does my behavior in respect of love effect nothing? That is because there is not enough love in me. Am I powerless against the untruthfulness and the lies which have their being all around me? The reason is that I myself am not truthful enough. Have I to watch dislike and illwill carrying on their sad game? That means that I myself have not yet completely laid aside small-mindedness and envy. Is my love of peace misunderstood and scorned? That means that I am not yet sufficiently peace-loving.

M—76

❧

WHERE there is power, there some result or other is produced. No ray of sunlight is ever lost, but the green which it wakes into existence needs time to sprout, and it is not always granted to the sower to live to see the harvest. All work that is worth anything is done in faith.   M—77

ALL the kindness which a man puts out into the world works on the heart and the thoughts of mankind, but we are so foolishly indifferent that we are never in earnest in the matter of kindness. We want to topple a great load over, and yet will not avail ourselves of a lever which would multiply our power a hundred-fold.

There is an unmeasured depth of truth in that strange saying of Jesus: "Blessed are the meek, for they shall inherit the earth" (St. Matt. v, 5).   M—78

AT THE station at Tarascon we had to wait for the arrival of our train in a distant goods shed. My wife and I, heavily laden with baggage, could hardly get along over the shingle between the lines. Thereupon a poor cripple whom I had treated in the camp came forward to help us. He had no baggage because he possessed nothing, and

I was much moved by his offer, which I accepted. While we walked along side by side in the scorching sun, I vowed to myself that in memory of him I would in future always keep a lookout at stations for heavily laden people, and help them. And this vow I have kept. On one occasion, however, my offer made me suspected of thievish intentions!

O—176

ON A stone on the river bank an old woman whose son had been taken sat weeping silently. I took hold of her hand and wanted to comfort her, but she went on crying as if she did not hear me. Suddenly I felt that I was crying with her, silently, towards the setting sun, as she was.

E—114

ANYONE can rescue his human life, in spite of his professional life, who seizes every opportunity of being a man by means of personal action, however unpretending, for the good of fellow men who need the help of a fellow man. Such a man enlists in the service of the spiritual and good. No fate can prevent a man from giving to others this

direct human service side by side with his
life work. 7   O—93

ANYONE who proposes to do good must
not expect people to roll stones out of his
way, but must accept his lot calmly if they
even roll a few more upon it. A strength
which becomes clearer and stronger through
its experience of such obstacles is the only
strength that can conquer them. Resistance
is only a waste of strength.   O—92

THAT everyone shall exert himself in that
state of life in which he is placed, to practice
true humanity toward his fellow men, on
that depends the future of mankind. Enor-
mous values come to nothing every moment
through the missing of opportunities, but
the values which do get turned into will and
deed mean wealth which must not be un-
dervalued. Our humanity is by no means so
materialistic as foolish talk is continually
asserting it to be. Judging by what I have
learned about men and women, I am convinced that there is far more in them of
idealist will power than ever comes to the

surface of the world. Just as the water of the streams we see is small in amount compared to that which flows underground, so the idealism which becomes visible is small in amount compared with what men and women bear locked in their hearts, unreleased or scarcely released. To unbind what is bound, to bring the underground waters to the surface: mankind is waiting and longing for such as can do that.   O—93-94

❧

CREATE for yourselves an auxiliary task, a simple and, if possible, a secret one. Open your eyes and try to see where a man needs a little time, a little sympathy, a little company, a little care. Perhaps he is a solitary, an embittered, a sick or an awkward man, to whom you can mean something. Perhaps he is an old man, perhaps a child. Who can enumerate all the possible uses of the valuable operating capital called man? He is needed in all parts. Therefore seek you for an opportunity to set your humanity to work. Do not avoid an auxiliary task, in which you give of yourself as man to other men. One is surely destined for you if you but really want it. K—254

❦

I GAVE up my position of professor in the University of Strasbourg, my literary work, and my organ-playing, in order to go as a doctor to Equatorial Africa. How did that come about?

I had read about the physical miseries of the natives in the virgin forests; I had heard about them from missionaries, and the more I thought about it the stranger it seemed to me that we Europeans trouble ourselves so little about the great humanitarian task which offers itself to us in far-off lands. The parable of Dives and Lazarus seemed to me to have been spoken directly of us! We are Dives, for, through the advances of medical science, we know a great deal about disease and pain, and have innumerable means of fighting them: yet we take as a matter of course the incalculable advantages which this new wealth gives us! Out there in the colonies, however, sits wretched Lazarus, the colored folk, who suffers from illness and pain just as much as we do, nay, much more, and has absolutely no means of fighting them. And just as Dives sinned against the poor man at his gate because for want of thought he never put himself in his place and let his heart and conscience tell him what he ought to do, so do we sin against the poor man at our gate.   E–1

❦

WE AND our civilization are burdened, really, with a great debt. We are not free to confer benefits on these men, or not, as we please; it is our duty. Anything we give them is not benevolence but atonement. For every one who scattered injury someone ought to go out to take help, and when we have done all that is in our power, we shall not have atoned for the thousandth part of our guilt. That is the foundation from which all deliberations about "works of mercy" out there must begin.   E–115-116

❦

IT WAS, and is still, my conviction that the humanitarian work to be done in the world should, for its accomplishment, call us as men, not as members of any particular nation or religious body.   E–2

§ 33

BUT ON one point he has an unerring intuition, and that is on the question whether any particular white man is a real, moral personality or not. If the native feels that he is this, moral authority is possible; if not, it is simply impossible to create it. The child of nature, not having been artificialised and spoilt as we have been, has only elementary standards of judgment, and he measures us by the most elementary of them all, the moral standard. Where he finds goodness, justice, and genuineness of character, real worth and dignity, that is, behind the external dignity given by social circumstances, he bows and acknowledges his master; where he does not find them he remains really defiant in spite of all appearance of submission, and says to himself: "This white man is no more of a man than I am, for he is not a better one than I am."

E—89

❧

BELIEVING it, as I do, to be my life's task to fight on behalf of the sick under far-off stars, I appeal to the sympathy which Jesus and religion generally call for, but at the same time I call to my help also our most fundamental ideas and reasonings. We ought to see the work that needs doing for the colored folk in their misery, not as a mere "good work," but as a duty that must not be shirked.   E–115

HOW can I describe my feelings when a poor fellow is brought me in this condition? I am the only person within hundreds of miles who can help him. Because I am here and am supplied by my friends with the necessary means, he can be saved, like those who came before him in the same condition and those who will come after him, while otherwise he would have fallen a victim to the torture. This does not mean merely that I can save his life. We must all die. But that I can save him from days of torture, that is what I feel as my great and ever new privilege. Pain is a more terrible lord of mankind than even death himself.

So, when the poor, moaning creature comes, I lay my hand on his forehead and say to him: "Don't be afraid! In an hour's time you shall be put to sleep, and when you wake you won't feel any more pain." Very soon he is given an injection of omni-pon; the doctor's wife is called to the hospital, and with Joseph's help, makes everything ready for the operation.

The operation is finished, and in the hardly-lighted dormitory I watch for the sick man's awakening. Scarcely has he recovered consciousness when he stares about him and ejaculates again and again; "I've no more pain! I've no more pain!" . . . His hand feels for mine and will not let it go. Then I begin to tell him and the others who are in the room that it is the Lord Jesus who has told the doctor and his wife to come to the Ogowe, and that white people in Europe give them the money to live here and cure the sick negroes. Then I have to answer questions as to who these white people are, where they live, and how they know that the natives suffer so much from sickness. The African sun is shining through the coffee bushes into the dark shed, but we, black and white, sit side by side and feel that we know by experience the meaning of the words: "And all ye are brethren" (Matt. xxiii, 8). Would that my generous friends in Europe could come out here and live through one such hour! E—62-63

WHETHER we will or no, all of us here live under the influence of the daily repeated experience that nature is everything and man is nothing. This brings into our general view of life—and this even in the case of the less educated—something which makes us conscious of the feverishness and vanity of the life of Europe; it seems almost something abnormal that over a portion of the earth's surface nature should be nothing and man everything!   E—101

TO BE prepared for confirmation I was sent to old Pastor Wennagel, for whom I had a great respect. But to him, too, I kept myself closely shut up. I was a diligent candidate, but the good man never suspected what was stirring in my heart. His instruction was in itself excellent, but it gave no answer to a great deal of what my inner self was concerned with. How many questions I would gladly have asked him. But that was not allowed us.

On one point—on that I was quite clear—my ideas differed from his in spite of all the respect I showed him. He wanted to make us understand that in submission to faith all reasoning must be silenced. But I was convinced—and I am so still—that the fundamental principles of Christianity have to be proved true by reasoning, and by no other method. Reason, I said to myself, is given us that we may bring everything within the range of its action, even the most exalted ideas of religion. And this certainly filled me with joy. M—42-43

❧

I FIND it no light task to follow my vocation, to put pressure on the Christian Faith to reconcile itself in all sincerity with historical truth. But I have devoted myself to it with joy, because I am certain that truthfulness in all things belongs to the spirit of Jesus. O—59

❧

"AS ONE unknown and nameless He comes to us, just as on the shore of the lake He approached those men who knew not who He was. His words are the same: 'Follow thou Me!' and He puts us to the tasks which He has to carry out in our age. He commands. And those who obey, be they wise or simple, He will reveal Himself through all that they are privileged to experience in His fellowship of peace and activity, of struggle and suffering, till they come to know, as an inexpressible secret, Who He is. . . ."   O—56-57

🍃

THE TRUE understanding of Jesus is the understanding of will acting on will. The true relation to Him is to be taken possession of by Him. Christian piety of any and every sort is valuable only so far as it means the surrender of our will to His.   O—56

🍃

I KNOW that I myself owe it to thinking that I was able to retain my faith in religion and Christianity.

The man who thinks stands up freer in the face of traditional religious truth than the man who does not, but the profound and imperishable elements contained in it he assimilates with much more effect than the latter.

The essential element in Christianity as it was preached by Jesus and as it is comprehended by thought, is this, that it is only through love that we can attain to communion with God. All living knowledge of God rests upon this foundation: that we experience Him in our lives as Will-to-Love.

O—238

❦

WHAT Christianity needs is that it shall be filled to overflowing with the spirit of Jesus, and in the strength of that shall spiritualize itself into a living religion of inwardness and love, such as its destined purpose should make it. Only as such can it become the leaven in the spiritual life of mankind. What has been passing for Christianity during these nineteen centuries is merely a beginning, full of weaknesses and mistakes, not a full-grown Christianity springing from the spirit of Jesus.

Because I am devoted to Christianity in deep affection, I am trying to serve it with loyalty and sincerity. In no wise do I undertake to enter the lists on its behalf with the crooked and fragile thinking of Christian apologetic, but I call on it to set itself right in the spirit of sincerity with its past and with thought in order that it may thereby become conscious of its true nature.

O—239-40

IN MY own life anxiety, trouble, and sorrow have been allotted to me at times in such abundant measure that had my nerves not been so strong, I must have broken down under the weight. Heavy is the burden of fatigue and responsibility which has lain upon me without a break for years. I have not much of my life for myself, not even the hours I should like to devote to my wife and child.

But I had blessings too: that I am allowed to work in the service of mercy; that my work has been successful; that I receive from other people affection and kindness in abundance; that I have loyal helpers, who identify themselves with my activity; that I enjoy a health which allows me to undertake most exhausting work; that I have a well-balanced temperament which varies little, and an energy which exerts itself with calmness and deliberation; and finally, that I can recognize as such whatever happiness falls to my lot, accepting it also as a thing for which some thank offering is due from me.

I feel it deeply that I can work as a free man at a time when an oppressive lack of freedom is the lot of so many, as also that though my immediate work is material, yet I have at the same time opportunities of occupying myself in the sphere of the spiritual and intellectual.

That the circumstances of my life provide in such varied ways favorable conditions for my work, I accept as something of which I would fain prove myself worthy.

O–242

MY MENTAL freshness I have, strange to say, preserved almost completely in spite of anaemie and fatigue. If the day has not been too exhausting I can give a couple of hours after supper to my studies in ethics and civilization as part of the history of human thought, any books I need for it and have not with me being sent me by Professor Strohl, of Zürich University. Strange, indeed, are the surroundings amid which I study; my table stands inside the lattice-door which leads on to the verandah, so that I may snatch as much as possible of the light evening breeze. The palms rustle an *obbligato* to the loud music of the crickets and the toads, and from the forest come harsh and terrifying cries of all sorts. Caramba, my faithful dog, growls gently on the verandah, to let me know that he is there, and at my feet, under the table, lies a small dwarf antelope. In this solitude I try to set in order thoughts which have been stirring in me since 1900, in the hope of giving some little help to the restoration of civilization. Solitude of the primeval forest, how can I ever thank you enough for what you have been to me? . . .

E—100

TWO perceptions cast their shadows over my existence. One consists in my realization that the world is inexplicably mysterious and full of suffering; the other in the fact that I have been born into a period of spiritual decadence in mankind. I have become familiar with and ready to deal with each, through the thinking which has led me to the ethical and affirmative position of Reverence for Life. In that principle my life has found a firm footing and a clear path to follow.

I therefore stand and work in the world as one who aims at making men less shallow and morally better by making them think.

O—219

THE TRUTH that the ethical is the essence of religion is firmly established on the authority of Jesus.   O–58

❦

A MAN is ethical only when life, as such, is sacred to him, that of plants and animals as that of his fellow men, and when he devotes himself helpfully to all life that is in need of help.   O–158-59

❦

ETHICS is the activity of man directed to secure the inner perfection of his own personality.   D–94

❦

CHRISTIANITY has need of thought that it may come to the consciousness of its real self. For centuries it treasured the great commandment of love and mercy as traditional truth without recognizing it as a reason for opposing slavery, witch burning, torture, and all the other ancient and medieval forms of inhumanity. It was only when it experienced the influence of the thinking of the Age of Enlightenment that it was stirred into entering the struggle for humanity.

The remembrance of this ought to preserve it forever from assuming any air of superiority in comparison with thought.   O—236

❦

LATE on the third day, at the very moment when, at sunset, we were making our way through a herd of hippopotamuses, there flashed upon my mind, unforeseen and unsought, the phrase, "Reverence for Life." The iron door had yielded: the path in the thicket had become visible. Now I had found my way to the idea in which affirmation of the world and ethics are contained side by side! Now I knew that the ethical acceptance of the world and of life, together with the ideals of civilization contained in this concept, has a foundation in thought.   O—156-57

❦

REVERENCE for Life arising from the Will-to-Live that has become reflective therefore contains affirmation of life and ethics inseparably combined. It aims to create values, and to realize progress of different kinds which shall serve the material, spiritual, and ethical development of men and mankind. While the unthinking modern acceptance of life stumbles about with its ideals of power won by discovery and invention, the acceptance of life based on reason sets up the spiritual and ethical perfecting of mankind as the highest ideal, and an ideal from which alone all other ideals of progress get their real value.

O—159-60

❦

TO AFFIRM life is to deepen, to make more inward, and to exalt the will-to-live.

At the same time the man who has become a thinking being feels a compulsion to give to every will-to-live the same reverence for life that he gives to his own. He experiences that other life in his own. He accepts as being good: to preserve life, to raise to its highest value life which is capable of development; and as being evil: to destroy life, to injure life, to repress life which is capable of development. This is the absolute, fundamental principle of the moral, and it is a necessity of thought.

O—158

❦

ANYONE who comes under the influence of the ethic of Reverence for Life will very soon be able to detect, thanks to what that ethic demands from him, what fire glows in the lifeless expression. The ethic of Reverence for Life is the ethic of Love widened into universality. It is the ethic of Jesus, now recognized as a logical consequence of thought. O—232

❦

THE CONCEPT of Reverence for Life has, therefore, a religious character. The man who avows his belief in it, and acts upon the belief, shows a piety which is elemental. O—235

❦

THROUGH Reverence for Life I raise my existence to its highest value and offer it to the world.

From the mysticism of Reverence for Life spring the drives to create and preserve the values which serve the perfection of man and mankind and the sum of which constitutes culture. S—88

❦

THE WILL to life that has become thought extends this behavior of Reverence for Life to all the will to life that comes within its range. This behavior makes man affirm life and the world and also makes him ethical. Ethics is not only behavior towards one's fellow men aimed at achieving a human society as happy and well ordered as possible. It is also the experience of a responsibility towards all living things, arising from an inner necessity.   S—38

❦

LIVING truth is that alone which has its origin in thinking.   O—223

❦

WITH its depreciation of thinking our generation has lost its feeling for sincerity and with it that for truth as well. It can therefore be helped only by its being brought once more on to the road of thinking.

Because I have this certainty I oppose the spirit of the age, and take upon myself with confidence the responsibility of taking my part in the rekindling of the fire of thought.   O—224

❦

NOT less strong than the will to truth must be the will to sincerity. Only an age which can show the courage of sincerity can possess truth which works as a spiritual force within it.

Sincerity is the foundation of the spiritual life. O—224

❧

BECAUSE I have confidence in the power of truth and of the spirit, I believe in the future of mankind. O—241

❧

IT IS not through learning about the world that we enter into a relationship with it but by experiencing it. Learning about the world can lead man only to a knowledge that everything that appears around him in time and space is essentially as much a will to life as he himself. The last knowledge turns to experience. S—38

❧

CIVILIZATION I define in quite general terms as spiritual and material progress in all spheres of activity, accompanied by an ethical development of individuals and of mankind. O—198

❧

HOW completely this want of thinking

power has become as second nature in men to-day is shown by the kind of sociability which it produces. When two of them meet for a conversation each is careful to see that their talk does not go beyond generalities or develop into a real exchange of ideas. No one has anything of his own to give out, and everyone is haunted by a sort of terror lest anything original should be demanded from him.   D—20

IT IS doubtful whether big cities have ever been foci of civilization in the sense that in them there has arisen the ideal of a man well and truly developed as a spiritual personality; to-day, at any rate, the condition of things is such that true civilization needs to be rescued from the spirit that issues from them and their inhabitants.   D—20-21

THE NEWEST scientific knowledge may be allied with an entirely unreflecting view of the universe.   D—72

BUT civilization can only revive when there shall come into being in a number of individuals a new tone of mind independent of the one prevalent among the crowd and in opposition to it, a tone of mind which will gradually win influence over the collective one, and in the end determine its charracter. It is only an ethical movement which can rescue us from the slough of barbarism, and the ethical comes into existence only in individuals.

D–73

❦

THE FINAL decision as to what the future of a society shall be depends not on how near its organization is to perfection, but on the degrees of worthiness in its individual members.

D–73

❦

THE EXISTING one is maintained by the Press, by propaganda, by organization, and by financial and other influences which are at its disposal. This unnatural way of spreading ideas must be opposed by the natural one, which goes from man to man and relies solely on the truth of the thoughts and the hearer's receptiveness for new truth. Unarmed, and following the human spirit's primitive and natural fighting method, it must attack the other, which faces it, as

Goliath faced David, in the mighty armor
of the age.   D—74-75

THAT is the condition in which we are
now, and that is why it is the duty of individuals to rise to a higher conception of
their capabilities and undertake again the
function which only the individual can per-
form, that of producing new spiritual-ethi-
cal ideas. If this does not come about in a
multitude of cases nothing can save us.

A new public opinion must be created
privately and unobtrusively.   D—74

THUS we tend to forget our relationship
with our fellows, and are on the path towards inhumanity. Wherever there is lost
the consciousness that every man is an object of concern for us just because he is man,
civilization and morals are shaken, and the
advance to fully developed inhumanity is
only a question of time.   D—24

AS A matter of fact, the most utterly inhu-
man thoughts have been current among us

for two generations past in all the ugly clearness of language and with the authority of logical principles. There has been created a social mentality which discourages humanity in individuals. The courtesy produced by natural feeling disappears, and in its place comes a behavior which shows entire indifference, even though it is decked out more or less thoroughly in a code of manners. The standoffishness and want of sympathy which are shown so clearly in every way to strangers are no longer felt as being really rudeness, but pass for the behavior of the man of the world. Our society has also ceased to allow to all men, as such, a human value and a human dignity; many sections of the human race have become merely raw material and property in human form.   D—24-25

THE NORMAL attitude of man to man is made very difficult for us. Owing to the hurry in which we live, to the increased facilities for intercourse, and to the necessity for living and working with many others in an overcrowded locality, we meet each other continually, and in the most varied relations, as strangers. Our circumstances do not allow us to deal with each other as man to man, for the limitations placed upon the activities of the natural man are so general and so unbroken that we get accustomed to them, and no longer feel our mechanical, impersonal intercourse to be something that is unnatural. We no longer feel uncomfortable that in such a number of situations we can no longer be men among men, and at last we give up trying to be so, even when it would be possible and proper. D–23-24

❦

EVERY being who calls himself a man is meant to develop into a real personality within a reflective theory of the universe which he has created for himself. D–93

❦

IN THIS way our own age, having never taken the trouble to reflect, arrived at the opinion that civilization consists primarily in scientific, technical and artistic achievements, and that it can reach its goal without ethics, or, at any rate, with a minimum of them. D–40

❦

THE DIFFICULT problems with which

we have to deal, even those which lie entirely in the material and economic sphere, are in the last resort only to be solved by an inner change of character. The wisest reforms in organization can only carry them to a little nearer solution, never to the goal. The only conceivable way of bringing about a reconstruction of our world on new lines is first of all to become new men ourselves under the old circumstances, and then as a society in a new frame of mind so to smooth out the opposition between nations that a condition of true civilization may again become possible. Everything else is more or less wasted labor, because we are thereby building not on the spirit, but on what is merely external.   D–60

❦

IF THE ethical is the essential element in civilization, decadence changes into renaissance as soon as ethical activities are set to work again in our convictions and in the ideas which we undertake to stamp upon reality. The attempt to bring this about is well worth making, and it should be worldwide.

It is true that the difficulties that have to be reckoned with in this undertaking are so great that only the strongest faith in the power of the ethical spirit will let us venture on it.   D—64

※

THE IDEA of the civilized man is none other than that of a man who maintains his humanity under all conditions. For ourselves it almost means to be civilized men if we maintain ourselves as men under the conditions of modern civilization.   K—266

※

THE FUTURE of civilization depends, therefore, on whether it is possible for thought to reach a theory of the universe which will have a more secure and fundamental hold on optimism and the ethical impulse than its predecessors have had.

D—96-97

※

LET US regard as valid only that which is compatible with humanity. . . . We hold high once more the sacred human rights, not those that the political rulers praise in their speeches and trample in their actions but the true ones. Once more we demand justice, not the one elaborated by lawyers deadened by juridical scholastics or that for which demagogues of all political shades shout themselves hoarse but a justice filled with the value of every human existence. The foundation of law is humanity. K–261

❦

WHEN in the spring the withered grey of the pastures gives place to green, this is due to the millions of young shoots which sprout up freshly from the old roots. In like manner the revival of thought which is essential for our time can only come through a transformation of the opinions and ideals of the many brought about by individual and universal reflection about the meaning of life and of the world. D–101

❦

THE WAYS along which we have to struggle toward the goal may be veiled in darkness, yet the direction in which we must travel is clear. We must reflect together about the meaning of life; we must strive together to attain a theory of the universe affirmative of the world and of life, in which the impulse to action which we experience as a necessary and valuable element of our being may find justification, orientation, clarity and depth, may receive a fresh access of moral strength, and be retempered, and thus become capable of formulating, and of acting on, definite ideals of civilization, inspired by the spirit of true humanitarianism.

D—105

Key to References

D — *The Decay and Restoration of Civilization.* London. Black, 1929.

E — *On the Edge of the Primeval Forest.* New York: the Macmillan Company, 1956.

K — *Aus meiner Kindheit und Jugendzeit.* Munich: Verlag C. H. Beck.

M — *Memoirs of Childhood and Youth.* New York: the Macmillan Company, 1955.

O — *Out of My Life and Thought.* New York: Henry Holt and Company, 1933.

S — *Selbstdarstellung.* Hamburg: Verlag Richard Meiner.

V — *Verfall und Wiederaufbau unserer Kultur.* Munich, C. H. Beck.